I0220364

DEGRADATION OF THE BLACK PEOPLE

IN THE 20th CENTURY

By Bernard A. N. Green.

DEGRADATION OF THE BLACK PEOPLE
IN THE 20th CENTURY

By Bernard A. N. Green.

Published & Copyright © 25/03/2021

Bernard A. N. Green

All rights reserved. No part of this book may be reproduced
in any form, by photocopying or by any electric or mechanical
means including information storage or retrieval systems, without
permission from the copyright owner and the publisher of this
book.

ISBN 978-0-9576042-7-8

Note. I want to show and describe the different forms of
degradation of the people of colour. But they were not the only
ones that suffered ridicule and abuse. I will show some of the
various forms that it took. Quite often it is in a surprising manner
and form.

TABLE OF CONTENTS

INTRODUCTION

THE COVER PICTURE

The above beautifully sculptured statue was supporting a table. I threw away the tabletop as he was hidden from view. I bought him in the 1980s but have no idea where or when he was created (probably in the 1950s). There were two of these supporting one large table-top, the other statue went to Jamaica.

MY CHILDHOOD

I am a white Englishman and when I was at school in the 1940s I was beaten by a male teacher by his fists because I could not memorize the arithmetic tables or remember the alphabet. A female teacher beat me with a horsewhip for not understanding what she was talking about, saying I was being difficult. What they did not understand that I was dyslexic and worse, I suffer dyscalculia which is that numbers and mathematics are a mystery to me. I was called a dunce and had to wear a conical white paper hat with a D on it, and in the classroom stand on a chair holding a sign- I AM A DUNCE. Of course, children can be quite nasty and tormented me but it made me learn to fight and I never lost in fisticuffs.

BENIN BRONZES

I was 12years old in 1946 when our male teacher showed us illustrations of the Benin Bronzes and told us that they were found in Africa. He informed us of their complexity and that it was not known how they were made. But he made a strong point of telling us that the Africans could not possibly have made them as they never had the technology. He then said they were probably made by Europeans that had lived there and had died out. This stuck in my mind and I made a point of searching for information on this subject later in my life.

The Benin Empire which occupied present-day Nigeria from the twelfth to the nineteenth century. The head of state was called the Oba and his palace was in Benin. Far from the ideas of many Europeans this society had an elaborate structure with a court that held ceremonials. These involved the chiefs, priests, warriors and palace societies which had guilds, foreign merchants, and mercenaries. The idea that mercenaries existed at that time might seem extraordinary but the information below from the National Geographic explains.

Bini. Also referred to as the Edo tribe. **Bini** people (derived from Benin) are found in Edo State in south Nigeria. They are descendants of the Benin Empire and speak Edo language, including several other dialects.

Benin's Power began to wane in the 1800s. They had civil wars and struggled to stop foreign traders.

The British politicians wanted to gain control over the Gold, Ivory, and slave trade. The British invaded Benin in 1897 and looted then burnt the City. The British then colonized the Kingdom making it part of British Nigeria. Nigeria gained its independence in 1960.

In the early modern era, Benin was also heavily involved in the West African slave trade. They would capture men, women, and children from rival peoples and sell them into slavery to European and American buyers. This trade provided a significant source of wealth for the kingdom.

www.nationalgeographic.org>encyclopedia>kingdom

Dahomey was an African Kingdom it developed in the 1600s and lasted until 1904 when the French invaded and the country was annexed into the French colonial empire. The capital is ABOMEY which is part of BENIN. The main language is FON.

THE RAF

Interestingly in 1955 I signed on for life in the RAF and enjoyed the atmosphere for a couple of months until one day the officers took us recruits into a classroom and said, "We are going to decide what you will do for the rest of your life". Green, what do you want to do? Fly said I! Ha-ha they laughed you have no A or O level Certificates of education. You cannot fly, try something else. "I would like to do diesel engineering Sir." "No, you will be GD," he said,

Soon it was lunch time and we walked to the Cookhouse, there was a rating digging a trench. I asked what his rating was "GD" he said. Then There was a chap cleaning the cookhouse drains, "What's your Rating" I asked, GD was the reply. When I got back to the class-room I told the officer "I am not doing GD." I was told I would be charged and may go to prison. I kept refusing General Duties! After two weeks a sergeant came to me and said pack your gear, you are going home, you are discharged and he gave me a rail ticket, I had to join the army as there was subscription in force.

But I joined The Royal Engineers for three years and thoroughly enjoyed it as I could go to classes without anybody taking the mickey out of me. I was a Corporal in the RE's and 22yrs old before I was told that I was Dyslexic and suffered Dyscalculia.

THE NORTH AND THE SOUTH

When I was 36 years of age I had a 50% share of a Yorkshire Quarry. I did all the right things like joining the Quarry-Men's Association but at the meetings I was called 'The Shit from London'!
And for no reason my Jaguar car was kicked all over so it looked like an orange. About this time which was 1970 I thought of living in Wales. I went to look at property and as I entered a public house it all went quiet as I spoke. This stopped me looking but I am glad as English people that bought houses there at that time had them burnt.

In human nature there has always been a friction and antagonism between different societies. And when a group or society has the power to do so, they often take advantage of the weaker group, tribe, society or religion.

The romans are the most obvious example, they had slaves, and killed Christians. The Arab nations traded in slaves and the Spanish empire brought nations to their knees in South America with massacres atrocities and slavery. I have not forgotten the British cruelty in its expansion of the Victorian British Empire and its involvement in the slave trade.

But do not forget that the Arabs and the Spanish dealt in slaves. And the more modern examples is the Nazi Regime in the way they dealt with the Jews. I find it sad that the way Israel treats the Palestinians means they did not learn from their past treatment by the Nazi regime. I wrote about this in a poem in 2012.

> The Warsaw Ghetto   (Haiku)
> Never again they all cry
> Gaza is Bombed.

ROMANI

The Romani, Romany, Gypsies or Travellers have had a particularly tough time that I have seen over my lifetime. That is from the 1940s. Prior to industrialization of farming I believe they had an interesting organized life moving from place to place depending on what crop needed picking. They worked in woodlands creating fencing and made other items for sale, basket work, brooms, birch tree faggots for the Bakers wood-fired ovens. There were plenty of other partime work opportunities such as tree felling and scrap collecting.

Those ovens are now long-gone and factories now produce thousands of items per day in plastic (which is not good for the environment). They had to adjust and many have gone into the building trade and made a great success of it, Due to these changes many have built their own houses. To do this requires a stable life. This anomaly is covered by the fact that they love the outdoor life, often keeping their caravans and horses. Their language is related to Hindi.

HINDI: **ROMANI/GYPSY:** *noun.* plural noun: gypsies a member of a people originating in South Asia and traditionally having an itinerant way of life, living widely dispersed across Europe and North and South America and speaking a language (Romani) that is related to Hindi; a Romani person. (Google)

But the general public do not wish to understand that people have different ideas and values and can be belligerent towards them. On the next page I will give you one example of what happened in our village, that I wrote about in a poem.

THE LONE TRAVELLER

As the light faded, the gypsy asked to camp
But the villagers gathered, to clap and stamp
We have to stop, or my poor horse will die
without rest, grass, and water. "No", they all cry

We won't have you here, lazy, work-shy
gipsies, people like you, go away, goodbye
Then she rode by; clippity clop. Does not dress up
or sat hunched like John Wayne, sits straight up

Head held high, hands and reins held down
always smiling, I've never seen her frown
She's never haughty, or shows distain
for mortals down on the muddy terrain

Her dog, a scruffy, muddy terrier
could not be happier, merrier
sitting still, on the rider's lap
Appears to smile, doesn't yap

Her bay mount, as cars pass by
does not worry, shimmy or shy
This lady has a natural rapport
apparent to all people rich or poor

This is, not only gained by being taught
but by observation and careful thought
The rider wheeled her fine steed around
studied the village group milling on the ground

Then, "Follow me young man", she loudly said
To her large village house, the pair she led
Next morning he tells her, "I am not a gypsy
I'm creating a film programme for the BBC".

―――――――――――

THE WIZARD COMIC

The Wizard was launched as a weekly British story paper on 22 September 1922, published by D. C. Thomson & Co.

SPADGER ISLE (1931-1950).

When I was a child aged 5yrs my father paid for a comic to delivered every week, it was called 'The WIZARD'. On the cover page every week, at the top was three or four pictures of an obese white man called 'Sam' and a young boy that he called 'Spadger'. Here they created the story-line for a large picture which showed that these two lived on an Island which was inhabited by people of colour.

Sam and Spadger had taken it upon themselves to teach these Island people how to do something different each week. As a child I found it amusing. The interior of the comic was always about white-men champions in cricket, football, cycling, and adventure stories. I did not read the football and cricket stories and have never become interested in football or cricket.

The Wizard comic was created by the publishing house D.C. Thomson who employed Charles Henry Gordon in 1922 as a staff artist. (Chick Gordon (1884-1952). He started with creating the one -panel cartoon called Cheery Chinks with the characters Spadger and Skipper Sam. This was 1922. The concept changed to Spadgers Isle in 1931. This is where they called the natives "Nigs" which shows a Victorian attitude or imagery.

The theme that runs through the whole period of the production was that the black people could not do anything efficiently and needed the white man to help and advise them. I do think that the politicians wanted to create this image in order to justify their territorial expansion across Africa and pretend to save the people from the hard existence in the jungle and re-educate them. This approach can still be seen applied in the 20th century in different nations.

The dialogue is extremely racist and degrading but in the years leading up to the 1940s was considered to be funny. This was probably seen the same way as the constant 'Irish' jokes that abounded. I have found that the main criticism of foreigners comes from people that have not travelled very much and therefore have a narrow outlook. People that have travelled and worked abroad have an insight into different cultures.

CHICK GORDON

By 1930 Gordon had taken over 'Spadger's XI', a kids' gang comic in The Wizard about a backyard soccer team, originally drawn by S.K. Perkins since 1925. The initial concept had worn out, and Gordon sent the two main characters on a trip around the world. They ended up on a deserted island, after which the comic›s title changed to 'Spadger Isle' (1931-1950). In true colonial fashion, Spadger and his companion, Skipper Sam, are quickly in charge of anglicizing the local tribe of cannibals, called the "Nigs". The comic was a product of its time, with the natives being drawn stereotypically and talking in jerky speech. The comic was popular enough to last through the 1930s and 1940s and moved from the centre-spread of Wizard to the front page on 28 October 1939, where it appeared in colour until 12 August 1950. Each page had a constant lay-out: four introduction panels and then one large, panel, in which all of the island's inhabitants and animals appear in comical situations related to that episode's subject.

Chick Gordon - Lambiek Comiclopedia

SPADGER ISLE

'Spadger Isle' started in the centre pages in 1931 and then moved to the frontpage on 28th Oct 1939. This feature was last illustrated on the No 1278 copy of the Wizard Comic on August 12th 1950. This showed trotting races being organized with zebra's instead of horses.

The Spadger Isle title became established in issue No 458 of September 12th 1931. It was inside printed in black and white until issue No 884 of November 11th

1939 when it became the cover page in full colour and stayed there until issue No 1278 of 12th August 1950.

There was a sudden change in the dialogue in the last four months of this long-lasting series. The No 1267 27th May 1950 was the last time the word 'Nigs' was used by Sam. On No 1268 'Old Timer' was used. No 1274 15th July 'Attention Folks'. No 1275 22nd July 1950 'Rastus and Sambo'. 1278 Aug 12th 'Rastus.

The Wizard Comic 1278 of Aug12th 1950 appeared to be the last issue showing 'Spadgers' Island. The following issue No 1279 August 19th.1950. At the top of the page, it states. Hi! LOOK! THE WIZARD HAS A NEW KIND OF COVER!
This cover article is a story about the young white British boys copying motorcycle speedway on their push-bikes.

However, I have seen three copies of THE WIZARD dated No 1564 February 4th 1956. - No 1570 March17th 1956. And No 1574 APRIL 14th 1956. All of which have Spadger Isle as the Front Cover. These are copies of earlier editions created by Chick Gordon with a few words changed and some colour changes. It appears to me that the comic might have been losing sales and this reversal might have been a bad attempt to revitalize the comic.

THEY TREATED US ROYALLY

It is obvious to me that the American Black soldiers coming to England to fight in the second World War started the change in the thinking of the Wizard comic's management.
Before the war, the black population of Britain was around 8,000 to 10,000 people.

An article that I read which I think has an important place in history is called "THEY TREATED US ROYALLY"? BLACK AMERICANS IN BRITAIN DURING WW2.

As it is a long article I do not wish to quote it but recommend that it is read. I will however quote a couple of items.

About 1.5 million Black American soldiers arrived in Britain who were mainly consigned to service and supply roles. But it was the black construction engineers that built the Airfields that are dotted all over Britain. These are where vast fleets of American bombers and fighters were launched and were instrumental in winning the war.

> *"They treated us royally"? The experiences of black Americans in Britain during the Second World War | Imperial War Museums (iwm.org.uk)*

Many of the leaders of the civil rights movement in the 1950s and 60s were veterans from the 2nd World War.

Something that puzzles me a great deal is that although I lived through the 2nd World War and a long time after I had never heard of the Black American pilots that defended America and Britain.

I have always been interested in aviation since a child, I had a spotter plane book in the war and a whole library of aviation books.

So why was there a dearth of information? Again, I think that politics stepped in.

ROHINGA. MYANMAR (FORMERLY BURMA)

The latest example of sectarian violence is the military taking power by the gun against the Rohinga Muslims and then the Buddhist populace. Shooting non violent men, women and children. The Chinese Government will not assist the people of Myanmar, they will assist the Army as they have invested heavily in industry in Myanmar.

19

ORDER YOUR "WIZARD" IN ADVANCE—AND MAKE SURE OF FOLLOWING UP THE S.X STAR STORIES INSIDE!
THE WIZARD
No. 905 APRIL 6TH 1940 PRICE 2D
LOOK, SERGEANT - YOUR APE BATTALION'S GOT LOOSE AMONG OUR PLANES, TANKS AND MOTOR BIKES! THEY'VE TAKEN THEM TO BITS AND TOMORROW WE'RE TO HAVE A REVIEW, BY THE MAYOR
GEE! I'M SORRY SKIPPER. I'LL GET THE APES TO PUT THEM MACHINES TOGETHER AGAIN AT ONCE!
WHAT A MESS.
PUT THOSE MACHINES TOGETHER AGAIN OR I'LL SKIN YOU ALL ALIVE!
AYE, AYE, SARGE!
SARGE CONGRATULATED ME ON PUTTIN' THE MACHINES RIGHT - LEASTWAYS HE SAID I'D ONLY GOT A SCREW LOOSE!
YEP! WE SURE MADE A JOB OF IT!
WE'D BETTER LAND HERE, PETE!
YEP, WELL, LOOK OVER THE MACHINE. THERE'S A LOOSE NUT OR TWO, I GUESS!
WOW! MY GORSH! THE APES HAVE MIXED THINGS UP PROPER!
HEY! COME BACK, YOU PALOOKAS! DON'T YOU KNOW YOU'RE THE BODYGUARD?
SURE WE DO SAH - WE'SE JUS' GONNA GUARD OUR BODIES!
LOOK SARGE, TANKS FLYIN' IN DE AIR. PLANES ROOTIN' UP HOUSES, AN' MOTOR BIKES CLIMBIN' TREES. DO YOH RECKON DIS AM DE END OB DE WORLD?
AH SURE KNOWS IT AM DE END OB DE APE BATTALION!
BETTER COME DOWN INTO DE BASEMENT, MISTER MAYOR!

22

NEW LAUGHS IN THE NEW YEAR WITH "THE SHERIFF WITH THE TWO-GUN TONSILS"
THE WIZARD
No 1015 JAN 9th 1943 PRICE 2D
JUMPIN' CATFISH, LOOK AT THAT NEW HOME GUARD OFFICER OF OURS. THAT LONG HAIR OF HIS IS A DISGRACE, AND A BAD EXAMPLE TO THE MEN.
WOW! THE MEN HAVE FOLLOWED HIS STYLE! BY GUM WE'VE GOT TO STOP THIS SPADGER. ORDER A GENERAL HAIR CUT PARADE TOMORROW.
ATTA BOY! AH SCYTHES ORF DE TOP-KNOTS AN' YOH CHOPS ORF DE SIDE BITS, SAMBO!
HELP! MAH EARS AM BEIN' CLIPPED ORF!
WHAT DID YOH SAY, CHUM? AH CAN'T HEAR - MAH EARS HAB GONE.
LAN' SAKES! DE SPRING OB DAT CHOPPER HAB GONE! GOOD-BYE PALS!
TOP-KNOTS CUT. SIDE BITS TRIMMED. NARROW SHAVES. SHAMPOO.
AH'LL DO YOH JUS' FOH EXPERIENCE, PAL. AH'M APPRENTICED TO DE HEDGE CUTTER!
FALL IN FOR HAIR CUTTING YOU BOYS. GET SMARTENED UP LIKE YOUR PAL HERE!
TAKE OUT A POLICY, SOLDIER. WE INSURE AGAINST LOSS OB ONE EAR, TWO EARS, OR ONE HEAD! CHEAPEST RATES!
STOP YOWLIN', FELLER. WE'LL GET YOH SOME HAIR-RESTORER AN' MEBBE EAR-RESTORER, TOO.
COME HERE RASTUS - FINISH OFF WITH A NICE SHAMPOO!
AH AINT HAVIN' NO SHAMPOO. AH JUS' HAD A HAIRCUT BY A SHAM BARBER WHO'S A EXECUTIONER IN DISGUISE!
DOCTOR AMOS, M.D.
SORRY LADY YOH GOTTA TAKE YOH CHILE TO DE VET OR SOME PLACE. MAH CONSULTIN' ROOM AM FULL OB FELLERS FROM DE BARBERS WID HALF DERE HEADS CUT ORF!

In the above picture which is No 1025 of May 29th 1943.
At the bottom left corner there is a blatant reference
to monkeys. which shows that certain people still had
a Victorian attitude in 1943 although Britain now
had approximately 1.5 million Black American troops
defending our country and attitudes were changing.

In this picture that 'Skipper Sam asks Rastus the enginneer to build a Bulldozer. But this is now 1944. Prior to this the everything the islanders did was innefective.

This appeared to be the last of the SPADGER'S ISLE
but it turns out it was not.

THE WIZARD

No 1279
AUG 19TH 1950
PRICE 2D

It all began among boys interested in motor-cycle speedway racing.

They found it possible to imitate on push bikes the methods of the motor-cyclists.

Bomb sites provided convenient spaces for these push-bike racers.

The tracks began to be cleared and marked out.

Teams with home-made uniforms raced in matches against each other.

THE STORY OF Cycle Speedway

NEARLY 300 CLUBS ARE MEMBERS OF THE NATIONAL CYCLE SPEEDWAY ASSOCIATION, AND THERE ARE HUNDREDS OF OTHER CLUBS THAT ARE AS YET UNREGISTERED.

Skilful riders began to find ways of improving their bikes for the new sport.

Leagues were formed with proper management committees, in which grown-ups gave a hand.

A well-known firm of cycle manufacturers put their designers on to the job of producing machines specially for cycle speedway.

Many of the teams showed enterprise in laying out proper tracks with concrete edging and rolled surfaces.

The sport is now well regulated, with proper leagues, in many towns all over Britain.

Cycle speedway is also popular in other countries. In Sweden races are held on ice-covered lakes.

31

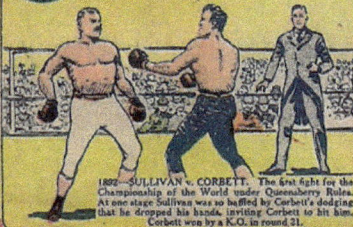
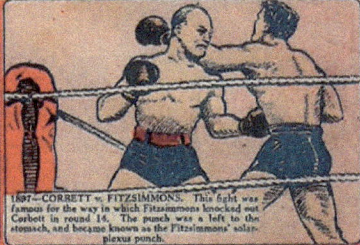

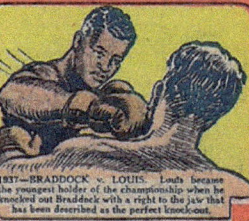

Here we have the No 1288 'WIZARD' of October 21st 1950.

It shows for the first time Jack Johnson's victory over Tommy Burns in 1908. And the victory of Joe Lois over Jim Braddock in 1937.

In this edition the artist tries to make fun of Hobboes which in the English dictionary means men falling on hard times.

This did not continue as it was not found to be funny.

THE IRISH NAVVIES

The Irish Navvies, this was a term that was short for Navigators. This was used to describe the Irish men that built the canals that crisscrossed Britain, then they worked on the railways and the roads. They were not hobboes or tramps. The British often use the term Paddy's which is a slang word.

As a child my father's café was on the A31 main road and it was frequented by these mostly Irish workers. There were many men that that my father called tramps, this was a person that travelled from place on foot and asked for free food. Another term for them is a beggar. My father never refused to give them food as he had had a very difficult childhood.

THE UIGHARS

China is facing mounting criticism from around the world over its treatment of the mostly Muslim Uighur population in the north-western region of Xinjiang.

Rights groups believe China has detained more than a million Uighurs over the past few years in what the state defines as "re-education camps".

There is evidence of Uighurs being used as forced labour and of women being forcibly sterilised.

Ref. *https://www.bbc.co.uk/news/world-asia-china-22278037*

A BRONZE STATUE

The above beautifully sculptured statue was supporting a table. I threw away the tabletop as he was hidden from view. I bought him in the 1980s but have no idea where or when he was created (probably in the 1950s). There were two of these supporting one large table-top, the other statue went to Jamaica with a friend of mine.

THE ANNAMITES OF SOUTHERN VIETNAM

Do not get the idea that only the people whose ancestors were from Africa were treated badly. Below I show you a postcard of Annamiite people being held prisoner by the French that controlled the southern part of Vietnam which they called 'ANNAM'
This device was called a Cangue. The next three photos were taken between 1902 and 1939. I wrote about these people in my book SPIES IN VUNG TAU 1925-9120 Photos of Vietnam.

INDIGENOUS MEN OF SOUTH VIETNAM

This photo of the indigenous people of South Vietnam was taken in 1950. It indicates to me that they were healthy and happy before the French took control of Annam in South Vietnam. The French called them 'Mois' which was derogatory. This was only 71 years ago!

THE MOIS OF SOUTHERN VIETNAM

136. - Environs de SAIGON. - Famille de Mois

These indigenous people were called 'MOIS' by the French. There were nomadic tribes called Koho, Raglai, Rhade and Bru. They practiced slash and burn agriculture and hunted with crossbows.

THE MARCHAND MISSION

The **Marchand Mission** was an expedition undertaken by French emissary Jean-Baptiste Marchand (1863-1934) and 150 men with designs to expand French colonial power in northeastern Africa. Starting from Libreville (in present-day Gabon) in 1897, the Marchand expedition spent 14 arduous months crossing largely uncharted regions of north central Africa. They finally reached the fort of Fashoda on the upper Nile on July 10, 1898 and hoisted the French flag. On September 18, a flotilla of five British gunboats led by Horatio Kitchener arrived at Fashoda; Kitchener had just defeated Mahdi forces at The Battle of Omdurman, and was in the process of reconquering the Sudan in the name of the Egyptian Khedive. The confrontation of the French and British was cordial but both sides insisted on right to Fashoda.

News of the encounter was relayed then to Paris and London and each side accused the other of expansionism and aggression. A stalemate (the Fashoda Incident) continued until November 3 when French Foreign Minister Théophile Delcassé, fearing the possibility of war, withdrew Marchand and his troops and ceded the Sudan to the British.

Wikipedia

BATTLE OF OMDURMA. 2nd September 1898. This is a fascinating true story of British and French territorial and economic expanionism into Africa. Winston Churchill was aged 25 when he fought at the Battle of Omdurman. Half of the 52,000 Dervish Army was killed by the use of the rifle and heavy artillery.

Thereby reconquering the Sudan. It is interesting that the Egyptian-Sudanese forces assisted the British in this battle.

British General Sir Herbert Kitchener was made Baron Kitchener of Khartoum following the battle.

FASHODA

Fashoda was in Egyptian Sudan. It is now named Kodok, South Sudan. General Kitchener claimed the whole of the Nile Valley for Gt Britain.

MISSION MARCHAND

RÉPRESSION A BRAZZAVILLE
Août 1896

EDITION DE LA TRAPPE DE N.D. D'AIGUEBELLE (Drôme)

MISSION MARCHAND

COMBAT DE M'TILA-VOULA
Janvier 1897

EDITION DE LA TRAPPE DE N.D. D'AIGUEBELLE (Drôme)

MISSION MARCHAND

ARRIVÉE A FASHODA
10 Juillet 1898

EDITION DE LA TRAPPE DE N.D. D'AIGUEBELLE (Drôme)

MISSION MARCHAND

HALTE DANS LE BAHR-EL-GAZAL
Juin 1897

EDITION DE LA TRAPPE DE N.D. D'AIGUEBELLE (Drôme)

LANTERN SLIDES

Lantern slides were invented in 1849' this was after the invention of photography'. They were glass pictures which could be projected onto a large screen.

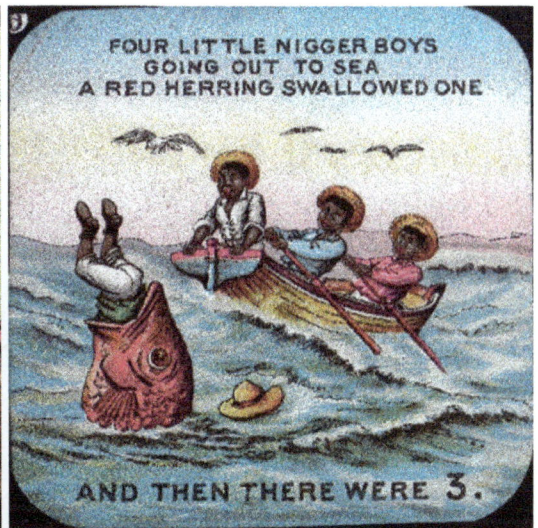

The above pictures are lantern slides from the 1800s which illustrated the story of Ten Little Nigger boys. This was still a popular story in children's books in the 1930s-1940s when I was a child. There were many versions.

Black dolls were very popular and there were many children's books with the theme of gollywogs being the nice guy or amusing as in the Florence Upton stories and pictures.

My favorite book was Robinson Crusoe., he had a man-servant that he named Man Friday. The other favorite of mine was The Mogli Stories which was about a boy that lived with the animals in the jungle.

ROBERTSON'S GOLDEN SHRED ENAMEL BADGES

These Enamel badges were created by the Golden Shred Jam and Marmalade Company called Robertson's to advertise their marmalade. The Ltd Company was established in 1903 after Mrs. Robertson had started making this clear marmalade that had a tangy taste from Seville oranges. This became very popular for breakfast when spread on toast. The company was awarded a Royal Warrant, initially by King George V in 1933, and subsequently by both King George VI and Queen Elizabeth.

The Silver Shred Marmalade was introduced in 1909 and had a sign created which said, SILVER SHRED Lemon Marmalade with capitals stating- GOLLY IT'S GOOD.

I will point out that at the time, the expression "Golly" was a common form of expression similar to saying "Gosh".

The Robertson's Golliwog symbol which appeared in 1910, is not politically correct and is seen as disrespectful and insulting. But we must remember that the founder James Robertson was born in 1832 and started in business in 1859. This was in the reign of Queen Victoria and the British had annexed the Cape Colony (South Africa) in 1815 where there were 25,000 Slaves.

The British Government were sponsoring settlers to emigrate to South Africa starting in 1820. So the times and thinking were very different.

THE 2nd WORLD WAR

The 2nd World War began to have an effect on attitudes. This was very obvious when the American troops arrived in Britain. Whereas the white Americans catcalled and ridiculed the Black American troops the British folks made them welcome.

I reproduce an article from the Tuskegee University as it really impressed me.

TUSKEGEE UNIVERSITY AIRMEN

- The Tuskegee Airmen were dedicated, determined young men who volunteered to become America's first Black military airmen

- Those who possessed the physical and mental qualifications and were accepted for aviation cadet training were trained initially to be pilots, and later to be either pilots, navigators, or bombardiers.

- Tuskegee University was awarded the U.S. Army Air Corps contract to help train America's first Black military aviators because it had already invested in the development of an airfield, had a proven civilian pilot training program and its graduates performed highest on flight aptitude exams.

- Moton Field is named for Tuskegee University's second President, Dr. Robert R. Moton who served with distinction from 1915-1935. The Airmen were deployed during the presidential administration of Dr. Frederick Douglas Patterson (1935-1953).

- The all-Black, 332nd Fighter Group consisted originally of four fighter squadrons, the 99th, the 100th, the 301st and the 302nd.

- From 1941-1946, some 1,000 Black pilots were trained at Tuskegee.

- The Airmen's success in escorting bombers during World War II – having one of the lowest loss records of all the escort fighter groups, and being in constant demand for their services by the allied bomber units.- is a record unmatched by any other fighter group.

- The 99th Squadron distinguished itself by being awarded two Presidential Unit Citations (June-July 1943 and May 1944) for outstanding tactical air support and aerial combat in the 12th Air Force in Italy, before joining the 332nd Fighter Group.

- The 332nd Fighter group was awarded the Presidential Unit Citation for its' longest bomber escort mission to Berlin, Germany on March 24, 1945. During this mission, the Tuskegee Airmen (then known as the 'Red Tails') destroyed three German ME-262 jet fighters and damaged five additional jet fighters.

- The 332nd Fighter Group had also distinguished itself in June 1944 when two of its pilots flying P-47 Thunderbolts discovered a German destroyer in the harbour of Trieste, Italy.

- The tenacious bomber escort cover provided by the 332nd "Red Tail" fighters often discouraged enemy fighter pilots from attacking bombers escorted by the 332nd Fighter Group.

- C. Alfred "Chief" Anderson earned his pilot's license in 1929 and became the first Black American to receive a commercial pilot's certificate in 1932, and, subsequently, to make a transcontinental flight.

- Anderson is also well known as the pilot who flew Eleanor Roosevelt, wife of then-U.S. President Franklin D. Roosevelt, convincing her to encourage her husband to authorize military flight training at Tuskegee.

- In 1948, President Harry Truman enacted Executive Order No. 9981 - directing equality of treatment and opportunity in all of the United States Armed Forces, which in time led to the end of racial segregation in the U.S. military forces.

- The U.S. Congress authorized $29 million in 1998 to develop the Tuskegee Airmen National Historic Site, with the University, Tuskegee Airmen Inc. and the National Park Service serving as partners in its development. To date, a mere $3.6 million has been appropriated for the Site's implementation.

Facts provided by Tuskegee Airmen Inc. and the Tuskegee University Office of Marketing and Communications.

RED BALL EXPRESS

The **Red Ball Express** was a famed truck convoy system that supplied Allied forces moving quickly through Europe after breaking out from the D-Day beaches in Normandy in 1944. To expedite cargo shipment to the front, trucks emblazoned with red balls followed a similarly marked route that was closed to civilian traffic. The trucks also had priority on regular roads.

Conceived in an urgent 36-hour meeting, the convoy system began operating on August 25, 1944. Staffed primarily with African-American soldiers, the Express at its peak operated 5,958 vehicles that carried about 12,500 tons of supplies a day. It ran for 83 days until November 16, when the port facilities at Antwerp, Belgium, were opened, enough French rail lines were repaired, and portable gasoline pipelines were deployed.

Use of the term "Red Ball" to describe express cargo service dated at least to the end of the 19th century. Around 1892, the Santa Fe Railroad began using it to refer to express shipping for priority freight and perishables. Such trains and the tracks cleared for their use were marked with red balls. The term grew in popularity and was extensively used by the 1920s.

The need for such a priority transport service during World War II arose in the European Theater following the successful Allied invasion at Normandy in June 1944. To hobble the German army's ability to move forces and bring up reinforcements in a counter-attack, the Allies had preemptively bombed the French railway system into ruins in the weeks leading up to the D-Day landing.

After the Allied breakout and the race to the Seine River, some 28 Allied divisions needed constant resupply. During offensive operations, each division consumed about 750 tons of supplies per day, totaling about 21,000 tons in all. The only way to deliver them was by truck – thereby giving birth to the Red Ball Express.

At its peak, it operated 5,958 vehicles and carried about 12,500 tons of supplies per day. Colonel Loren Albert Ayers, known to his men as "Little Patton, was in charge of gathering two drivers for every truck, obtaining special equipment, and training port battalion personnel as drivers for long hauls. Able-bodied soldiers attached to other units whose duties were not critical were made drivers. Almost 75% of Red Ball drivers were black.

Red Ball Express. From Wikipedia, the free encyclopaedia.
Page Version ID: 1000156830. Wikipedia.

THE BRITISH BLACK SOLDIERS PAY

A document discovered at the Kew Archives by the News program Aljazeera for its program-English People on its Power Series. Britain paid its soldiers by rank, service and colour of their skin.

British soldiers received a war gratuity. It is known that Kenyan soldiers that served in Burma did not receive the War Gratuity.

White Corporals received a war gratuity of 12 Shillings per month of service.
The Black corporals received 4 shillings per month!
A white private could earn 10 shillings for each month of service. With only 3.5 shillings for a Black person.

Europeans received per month-

Private	10/- (10 Shillings)
Corporal	12/-
Sergeant	14/-
Staff/Sergeant	16/-
W.O 11.	18/-
W.O. 1.	20/-

AFRICAN SOMALI RANKS

African Somali ranks received per month

Private	3.5 Shillings
Corporal	4/-
Sergeant	4.5 Shillings
S/Sergeant	5/-
W.O.11.	5.5 Shillings
W.O.1.	6/-

Women of the East African Forces including Nursing Officers Received two-thirds of the male ranks.
Mauritian and Seychellois women received half.
Asian personnel received 7.5shillings for each months enlisted irrespective if their rank.

A BRITISH BOYS GRAMMAR SCHOOL

Grammar schools have existed since the 16th Century, but the modern grammar school concept dates back to the Education Act 1944. This made secondary education after the age of 14 free. Grammar schools, focused on academic studies, with the assumption that many of their pupils would go on to higher education.

I have copied three articles from a Surbiton Grammar School dated 1965. This Grammar school closed down in 1965. So this was the last Albury house magazine.

There were 28 articles in this document of thirty-one pages. Most are jocular, a couple are on architecture. The first one that I have copied is on page 26 and entitled NAT 'KING' COLE.
It is a pleasant article about Nat King Cole who died of cancer on the 15th February 1965. The writer wrote of the Negro vocalists' rendering of such songs as 'Nature Boy', 'Too Young', 'Rambling Rose', 'Unforgettable', and 'Somewhere Along the Way'.
Eventually he had the foundation of a show business empire. He also owned a film production company. In 1937 he was a piano vocalist in small night clubs until he formed the 'KING COLE BAND'.

IT'S CALLED A COLOUR PROBLEM. This is the second story I have copied from pages 12-13. It relates the story of a Black American that moved to Memphis to practice his music and discovered that his presence was not wanted in the local White dominated restaurants.

NAT 'KING' COLE

Nat 'King' Cole died of cancer in California on the 15th February 1965 at the age of only 45. Although he was not so popular in Europe he was one of America's most popular artists. His throaty baritone earned him the nickname of 'The Sound'.

The Negro vocalist's husky rendering of such songs as 'Nature Boy', 'Too Young', 'Rambling Rose', 'Unforgetable', and 'Somewhere along the way' eventually became the foundation of a show business empire. He also owned a film production company.

He was born in Alabama, son of Rev. Edwards Coles. He recieved his early musical education from his mother at the age of Nine. While a student in Chicago, he organised his own band. In 1937 he worked as piano vocalist in small night clubs until he formed 'King Cole Trio' band.

Cole was first married to a dancer, Nadine Robinson in 1937. This marriage was dissolved in 1946 and two years later he married Marie Ellington, also a singer. They had four daughters and an adopted boy.

IT'S CALLED COLOUR PROBLEM

Jeff occupied a small room in one of the Negro sections of Memphis, Tennessee that is, where it was only possible for him to sleep and sing his Blues songs that he had written. It was a simple life and he did not complain. What was there to complain about? He got his food from his landlady and he enjoyed his work, although the pay was not particularly high. He very seldom went out in the evenings and even when he did it was only to the cafe down the road.

After one of his monthly payments, he decided to have a fling and try a new place to go and eat. So that evening he took the bus into the centre of the city and started his hunt for a suitable-looking place. The first restaurant he tried he got a polite but heart-burning reply that they did not serve Negroes. He tried not to be put off by this remark but every other restaurant he went to, he seemed to lose his nerve to go in and find out whether or not he would be served.

At last he built up enough courage and he went into a rather shabby-looking restaurant and sat down at a side table. Nobody seemed to want to serve him but at last a waiter came up and gave him

13
the menu. He quickly ordered the cheapest and simplest meal on the card and then just sat still trying to ignore the majority of the people in the place who were staring at him.

He got back to his little room about an hour later and before he did anything he started chuckling to himself for being such an idiot to try and mix with people not of his own kind.

54

A MODEST PROPOSAL

The third story is truly shocking and quite impossible to understand the thinking of the writer. This article was written with a bitterness and anger which is impossible to comprehend.

Although I believe in free speech I cannot understand how and why the headmaster allowed this to be printed as it would have been controversial in 1965. But the school closed in this year, perhaps there was too much happening with students moving to other schools. Until 1965 the school was on Surbiton Hill Road in Surbiton. The three main buildings were large Victorian mansions called Braemar (where pupils began their school lives), Aysgarth and Albury.

These articles were in the Albury House Magazine and would have been the last edition.

Surbiton is a suburban neighbourhood of south-western Greater London, within the Royal Borough of Kingston upon Thames.

I have sent the magazine to the Smithsonian National African American Museum 1400 Constitution Ave. NW, Washington, DC 20560, United States.

23

A MODEST PROPOSAL

With sincere apologies to Jonathan Swift Esq., author and poet.

It is agreed by all that one of the major social problems of our era is that which arises when white men and black men come into contact and have to share the same jobs and living conditions; there is inevitably, wherever this may happen, friction or open hostility which leads to the detriment of all concerned. Many solutions have been attempted: general agreements, segregation, apartheid, subjection and so on. Mine is only a modest proposal, but one, I assure you, that would work to the happiness and contentment of as many person's as possible.

My suggestion is this; that a very large percentage of Black men and women should be subjected to the treatment of battery hens. Let me expand, for this has a twofold purpose. The tenderest, probably those of the female sex, would be singled out at birth and given merely half the treatment; when they reached the age of about two or three they would then provide a succulent dish, befitting the table of a king, more dainty and tender a morsel than a mouthful of young chicken: this, I have heard from my South African friend, is perfectly true. The other half would be given the full treatment and would, having reached full maturity at an age of about ten years old, be sent to work as mules, pack horses or some other instruments of useful manual labour for which negroes are si well known.

A limited number, the strongest and healthiest at birth, would escape this process, for they would be necessary for the purpose of breeding. The battery negroes, you see, will be fertilised at birth so as to give their muscles more scope in which to grow unimpeded. The breeding negroes will be separated from the others and allowed to grow up of their own accord, in wired reservations, or hutches; by my computation it will be necessary to allow five or six breeding females to one breeding male, and this in three years, over twenty children would be produced by each breeding male, of which the majority will go to the battery houses. Naturally, when the breeders have outlived their purpose, they will be slaughtered forthwith.

To return to the battery negroes. Having been suckled, they will be taken away from their mothers and removed promptly to a small hutch, absolutely hygenic to prevent germs from spreading; here, in solitary confinement so as to waste no energy on others, the negro will be fed, in the dark, on high grade nutrients, concentrated and in liquid form (as are chickens), until, if one of them is chosen, he or she will be removed after about three years, having attained the normal maturity of a normal child of ten.. The slaughtering before canning is, I assure you, quite hygenic; the negro is hung up by his legs on a conveyer belt, given a mild, stunning, electric shock, from which he passes on to have his throat cut before being plucked and dismembered. The other half of the battery blacks continue for five or six more years until they are physically fully grown; the negro is known for his strength and capacity of work, and so they can be harnessed to useful heavy manual labour, coal-mining, ploughing, or for the females, sanitary work. Of course, having been so forcefully reared, their strength will fail within two or so years, but still, they will be able to do invaluable services to the good of their fellow human-beings. When they become useless, they will be straightway slaughtered and either end their days as manure,

CRESTED CHINA

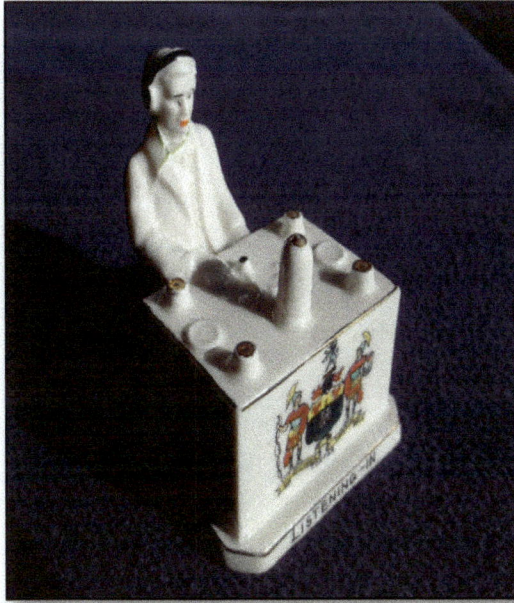

The radio operator

I will explain why this picture of a wartime 'RADIO OPERATOR' is here. Since the early 1900s these items were sold as mementos to remember events and holidays. Included in these there are numerous items whick are now called Black Boy Crested China which has become very collectable in Britain, I have noticed that one of them is a crocodile chasing a black boy. Apparently this was a popular theme for china mementos being sold in the everglades in Florida many years ago.

The 1985 price guide to Crested China by Sandy Andrews & Nicholas pine is an excellent guide to the china and lists over 24 different items of Black Boy China

BLACK BOY CRESTED CHINA

THE FOLLOWING ITEMS ARE CRESTED CHINA ITEMS THAT ARE LISTED AS BLACK BOY CRESTED CHINA - This is the title under the Ebay site.

Made of porcelain, it is vitrified pottery and was first made in China in the Tang Dynasty (618-907 AD). What is shown above was made in Britain between 1858 and 1940. There is a great interest these days in crested china that was made Durng the 1st World War. These are Tanks, Zeppelins, Aircraft, Searchlights and guns, There are numerous other items like Soldiers throwing hand-grenades, Zeppelin bombs and Shells, there is a Jack Johnson Artillery shell., named because it was so large. If you do not know who he was I will write something about him.

THE ABOVE ASSORTMENT OF CRESTED CHINA ARE ALL APPROX. 90 YEARS OLD.

JACK JOHNSON CRESTED CHINA ARTILLERY SHELL

There is a large Crested China artillery shell named the Jack-Johnson. In case you do not know who he was, he was born in 1878 and was the first African American to hold the World Boxing title. He was champion from 1908 to 1915.

He fought James J. Jeffries in Reno, Nevada on July 7th 1910. The fight ended in the 15th round when Jeffries admitted defeat.

He had a total of 73 victories, 13 losses and 10 draws,

He was convicted in 1913 by an all-white jury for violating the Mann Acton charges that he had transported a white woman across the state line 'for "immoral purposes." It was obviously racially motivated charges. He served 10 months of his one year sentence,

He died in 1946 aged 68.

Sylvester Stallone brought the case to the attention of President Trump who signed a pardon for Jack. Johnson on 24th May 2018.
Current Champion Deontay Wilder and Lennox Lewis CBE, CM. were also at the ceremony.

Deontay Wilder had a perfect record of 40 wins and no losses.

Crested china. Two children sitting on a log.

Crested china. Is'e making ink.

There are others made by Arcadia that are similar.

An assortment of dolls

On the previous page, an interesting two-headed doll.

An assortment of china. there are two crested china items at the back. the rest are not historical memorabilia. the two boys at the front left are salt and pepper shakers and the others are just ornaments.

This metal statue does not have a title but when I was young, about the 1940s-50s, the coalman who delivered bags of coal to the houses wore a hessian sack tied over his shoulders.

So, I think this chap was carrying coal which had sharp edges or bags of stone.

VICTORIAN SCRAP-BOOKS

Children for many years have had scrap books and collected in many themes. The ones below are from the Victorian era.

My scrap books were full of aircraft, British, German, and American.
They were still very popular in the 1940s. Mine were all full of aircraft, German British and American.

Other boys collecting themes were Footballers, Cricketers, Army regimental uniforms.

THIS STYLE OF DRESS WAS CALLED 'DANDY'S'

Quite often these scrap-book figures had to be cut out of sheets of paper that they were printed on. The printing was often done by the chromolithograph system which gave a very high quality of print.

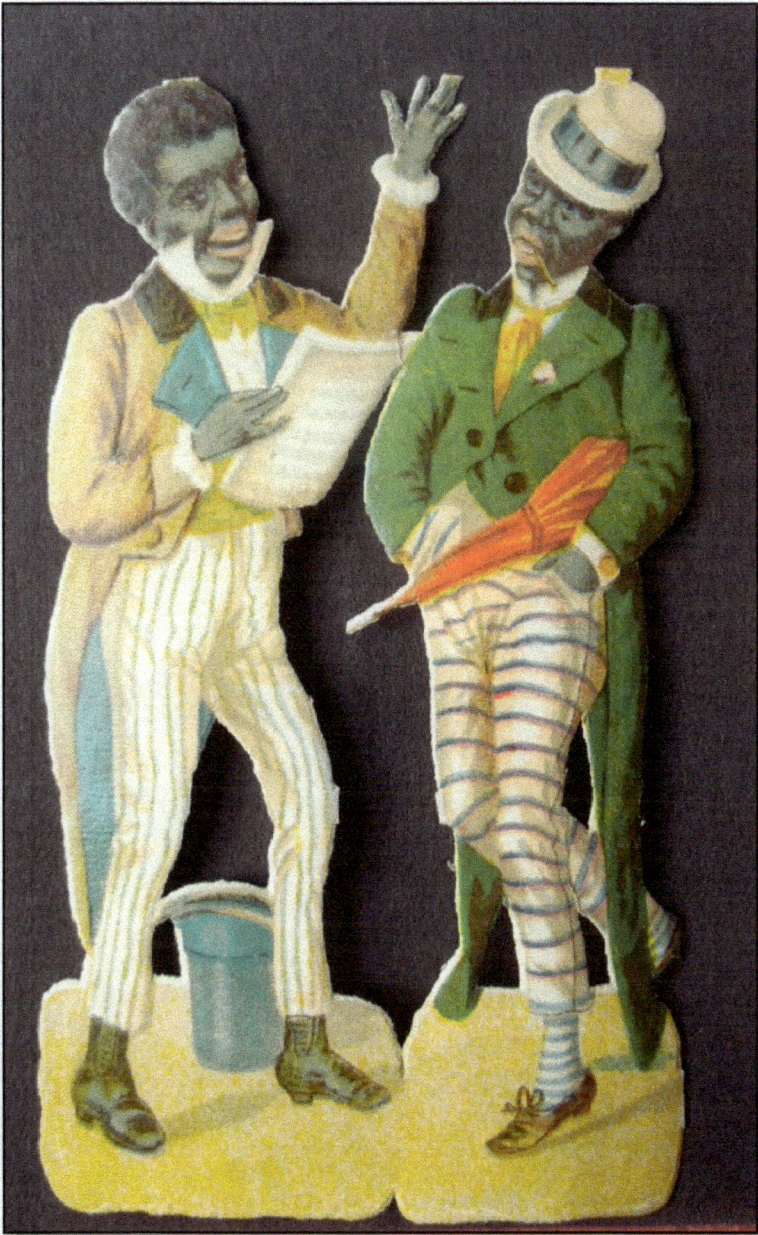

A Dandy was or is a man that places a high value on physical appearance with an appearance of nonchalance.

ADVERTISING CARDS

THIS CARD WAS ADVERTISING A FRENCH
RESTAURANT.

"CETICISM, MY BELOBED BREDREN, IT AM SOME...HING BEAUTIFUL FRINSTANCE
IT AM LIGHT AND AIRY ~ LIKE DE BEAN."

ELDERLY GENT:~"WHY DOES HE WANT TO SHINE 'EM UP FOR NUFFIN? SPECT DE
LITTLE NIGGER TINKS DEYD BE A BIG ADVERTISEMENT FOR HIM."

LIEBIG TRADE CARDS

These trade cards show the influence of the French and the opium trade that they helped expand in order to supply China.

Trade cards were used to advertise products and were usually very good at ridiculing political life.

Li, d'un coup de pépin lancé d'une main sûre,
Fit sur ce vilain monstre une large blessure.

Voir au verso.

VÉRITABLE EXTRAIT DE VIANDE LIEBIG.

N° 6. — Bon Noir défendra son bien contre petit Blanc.

Voir au verso.

The above three cards are a French trade card for Liebig which was a meat extract. They were very good at making fun but they also created many themes that are historically correct and collectable.

The No 7 card below LES BAYAKA is the first card on the next page.

Potages Liebig en boîtes : Tomate - Cerfeuil - Légumes - Oxtail - Crèmes Champignons et Asperges : la formule économique du "bien manger".

7. LES BAYAKA

Les Bayaka, au nombre de 180.000 environ, habitent le sud-ouest de la Province de Léopoldville, au voisinage de la grande rivière Kwango. Ils parlent la langue bantoue.

D'aucuns considèrent les Bayaka comme les descendants des farouches Jaca, qui envahirent la région au XVIe siècle, et dont les explorateurs portugais de l'époque font mention lorsqu'ils parlent de "troupes nomades, guerrières et anthropophages".

Actuellement, les Bayaka sont toujours de grands chasseurs ; ils pratiquent l'agriculture et se livrent aux menus métiers que réclament leurs besoins journaliers.

Ils sculptent le bois et en fabriquent des objets aux usages les plus variés : des masques de danse, polychromés, souvent garnis de barbes longues et touffues en raphia, et surmontés de figurines animales ou humaines dans des attitudes parfois inattendues ; ces masques servent aussi dans les sociétés d'initiation ; ils font encore des statuetttes, dont la figure s'orne souvent d'un nez caractéristiquement retroussé, des objets usuels divers tels que peignes sculptés, sifflets, épingles à cheveux, etc...

L'image représente un danseur coiffé d'un de ces masques volumineux ; deux autres genres de masques sont dessinés dans le bas, en même temps qu'une statuette au nez retroussé.

En médaillon, une tête de femme des Basuku, étroitement apparentés aux Bayaka, et habitant la même région.

Compagnie Liebig, fondée en 1865

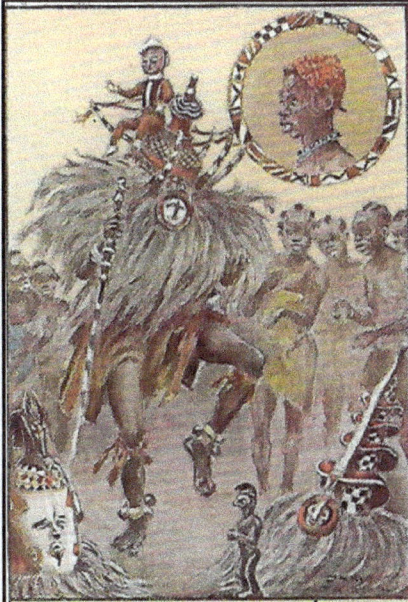

PEUPLADES DU CONGO BELGE
7. Les Bayaka
Cube de bouillon Liebig: force et saveur
Reproduction interdite   Explication au verso

PEUPLADES DU CONGO BELGE
8. Les Ngombe
Extrait de Viande Liebig: l'ami des gourmets
Reproduction interdite   Explication au verso

PEUPLADES DU CONGO BELGE
2. Les Batetela
Lemco Chicken Soup: pour manger mieux
Reproduction interdite   Explication au verso

PEUPLADES DU CONGO BELGE
3. Les Mangbetu
Extrait de Viande Liebig : l'ami des gourmets
Reproduction interdite   Explication au verso

PEUPLADES DU CONGO BELGE
9. Les Bushongo
Haricots à la Tomate Liebig: prêts à servir
Reproduction interdite   Explication au verso

PEUPLADES DU CONGO BELGE
10. Les Bambuti
Bouillon Oxo: véritable bouillon de viande
Reproduction interdite   Explication au verso

PEUPLADES DU CONGO BELGE
11. Les Wagenia
Lemco Chicken Soup: pour manger mieux
Reproduction interdite   Explication au verso

PEUPLADES DU CONGO BELGE
12. Les Azande
Produits Liebig: économie
Reproduction interdite   Explication au verso

PEUPLADES DU CONGO BELGE
13. Les Babali
Cube de bouillon Liebig: force et saveur
Reproduction interdite   Explication au verso

PEUPLADES DU CONGO BELGE
14. Les Arabisés
Haricots à la Tomate Liebig: prêts à servir
Reproduction interdite   Explication au verso

PEUPLADES DU CONGO BELGE
15. Les Wasongola
Extrait de Viande Liebig : l'ami des gourmets
Reproduction interdite   Explication au verso

PEUPLADES DU CONGO BELGE
16. Les Bangelima
Bouillon Oxo: véritable bouillon de viande
Reproduction interdite   Explication au verso

POWER OF THE GUN

Power is the problem. First the fist then the club, then the spear followed by the bow and arrow, cross-bow and the gun.
Now the availability of the gun and explosives has caused the whole world in a state of war.

Now there is a change to cyber war. Instead of using politics to mock or deprecating people, governments are using cyber war as economic warfare on industries and countries.

The people with power will always take advantage of the weak or attempt to do so. It is so in the case of with every society and country.

The weak are seen as pawns, people to be used or manipulated, sometimes just to make fun of!
I have experienced this division of society. I went to a comprehensive Secondary school and left without any 'O' levels or grades as in the USA. However after serving in the Royal Engineers I purchased my father's transport café that was called Alf's Café on the main London to Portsmouth A 31 road.
I was able to turn it into a renowned café, with stories published about it on the London Grip internet magazine.

I purchased a house in a nearby village which is in an area of outstanding beauty. I was told more than once that "You should not be in this village as you are just a common café owner"!

They said the village was for educated people but what they did not know was that I owned a coffee bar, had founded the first Skydiving school in the UK and as worked as coordinator-skydiver in a Steve McQueen and James Bond film. I also owned a York Stone Quarry, but I could not be bothered to talk to people with that attitude.

HISTOIRE DU CONGO BELGE (1ᵉ partie)
3. Stanley (1841-1904) — Découverte du cours du fleuve Congo
POTAGE CREME LIEBIG „CHAMPIGNONS": un régal pour les palais délicats

At my school I was taught that Stanley was a wonderful man who was an explorer, cartographer, and educator.

I was surprised to find that Henry Martin Stanley was sent by Belgiums's Leopold the 2nd to the Congo region between 1869-1874. He made treaties with African Chiefs and by 1882 had enough territory to create the CONGO FREE STATE. That sounds nice doesn't it. Leopold the 2nd personally owned the colony and it was used as a source of rubber and ivory. He owned an area approximately 75 times larger than Belgium.

The Congo Free State imposed a reign of terror on the people.

I have seen photos of the labourers, women and children that had their hands cut off for not meeting their rubber collection quotas.
I write this to try and explain the mindset in the 1800s which was truly wicked.

ANEXATION OF THE TERRITORY OF THE KING OF ADO

ANNEXATION OF THE TERRITORY OF THE KING OF ADO (1891).

Here we see the British Empire in the actual process of extension. Captain G. C. Denton, now the Colonial Secretary of Lagos, on the Bight of Benin, is taking over from his Majesty the King of Ado the sovereignty of his dominion, which henceforward will be administered, greatly to its advantage, under the British flag. The King may be observed in the regalia suitable to so important an occasion, and overshadowed by the Umbrella of State. Captain Denton and his staff, including a naval and a military officer, are in costumes not usually associated with the splendours of a court, but none the less serviceable on that account. The men of Ado, who occupy the foreground, have clearly learnt to understand the nature of a photographic camera, and have evidently just received from the operator the familiar instruction to "look pleasant."

Photo : N. Walwin Holm, F.R.P.S., Lagos.

This was 1891. Annexation by the British Empire. You will notice the Military presence and the man with the gun. On the next page are French trade cards advertising chocolate for LE Monastere- d'Aiguebelle. Date 1893. I turned the picture to make it easier to see.

81

Édité par la
CHOCOLATERIE DE N. D. D'AIGUEBELLE
(Drôme)

Campagne du DAHOMEY (1893)
Attaque du camp de Dogba par les Dahoméens

Imprimé pour la
CHOCOLATERIE D'AIGUEBELLE
Monastère de la TRAPPE (Drôme)

Campagne du DAHOMEY (1893)
Attaque du camp de Dogba par les Dahoméens

Nº 46.   Campagne du DAHOMEY. Attaque du camp de Dogba
19 Septembre 1893

Au commencement de 1893 nos possessions du Dahomey étaient compromises. Behanzin, le roi de ce pays, en dépit des traités qu'il avait signés avec nous, menace de s'emparer de Whydah et de Porto-Novo.

Le gouvernement Français organise une expédition sous le commandement du colonel Dodds, de l'infanterie de marine, afin de châtier ce roi rebelle.

Le 29 Mars 1893 cette expédition arrive à Kotonou. Le colonel Dodds marche directement sur Abomey, capitale du Dahomey. Il se fraye une route à travers les bois et les marécages. Partout il rencontre des embuscades et craint à chaque instant d'être surpris.

Le 19 Septembre 1893, malgré le guet attentif de nos sentinelles, les Dahoméens débouchent à l'improviste dans notre camp de Dogba. Nos soldats sont de suite prêts et résistent à l'attaque sans faiblir.

Dans cette escarmouche nous perdons malheureusement le commandant Faurax qui, à la tête de la légion étrangère, avait achevé la déroute de l'ennemi.

Le Monastère de N.-D. d'Aiguebelle, fondé en l'an 1045, est situé dans une vallée solitaire du Canton de GRIGNAN (Drôme). La célébration de l'OFFICE DIVIN, le TRAVAIL DES MAINS et L'ÉTUDE se partagent la journée du trappiste. Le TRAVAIL MANUEL est de nos jours, pour les religieux de la Trappe, non seulement un point de règle, mais une nécessité absolue. Leurs seules ressources proviennent, en effet, de l'exploitation agricole et plus spécialement de la fabrication du CHOCOLAT D'AIGUEBELLE.

BELGIAN CONGO

Belgian Congo postcard circa 1900. 5 Centimes stamp.
The populace enjoying the fruits of annexation.

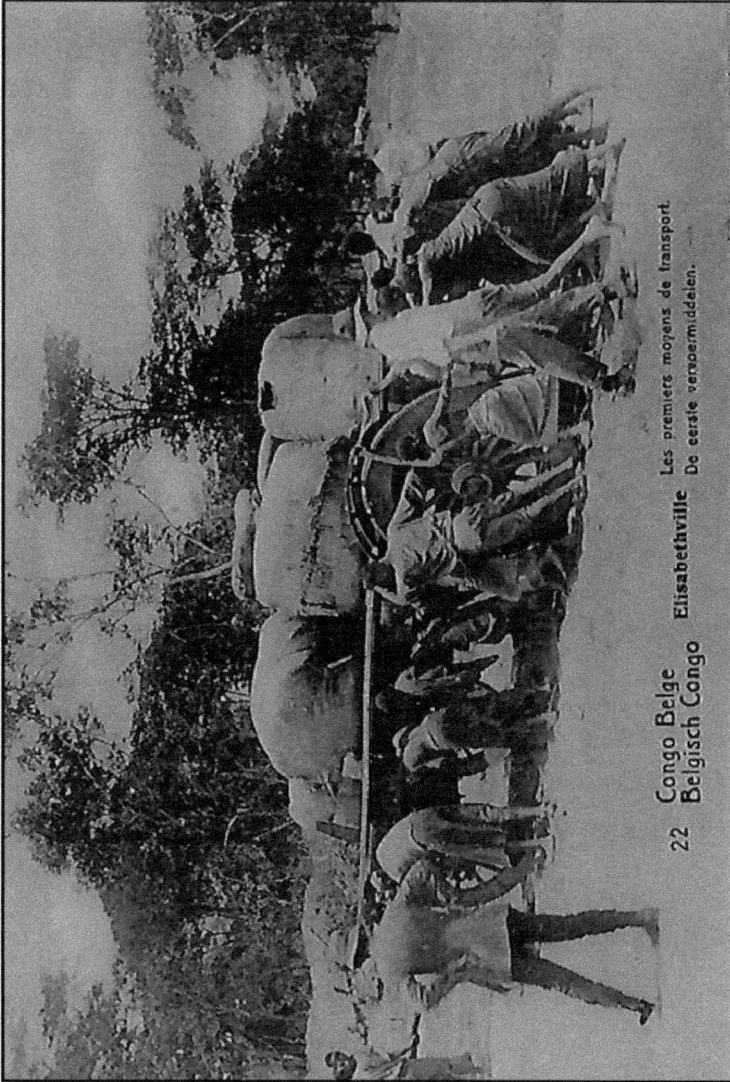

Belgian Congo. Postcard posted 1910. Elizabethville,
Premier transport! European technology!

THE PYGMIES

BOKANE (CHIEF). MAFUTIMINGA. MATUKA.
QUARKE (PRINCESS). MONGONGA. AMURIAPE.

Photo Gale & Polden, Ltd.

This has a date of August 1887. These Pygmies were on display at Earl's Court Exhibition in London. The title was Pygmies from the Dark-Forest of Africa.

POST CARDS

British John Bull standing outside the Tower of
London.
What looks like a politician is using a 'Road Tamper to
tamp down FREE TRADE. This most probably meant
free trade with Africans.
It was postcard was posted in 1907.

I do believe that the humble postcard was used as a
political weapon.

Below are postcards from various countries, The
next card is particularly shocking. If you study the
scene that it depicts, The man being kicked is a Black
American. The boot obviously belongs to a white man.
The daughter is in the window showing distress.

MAY YOU THOROUGHLY ENJOY YOURSELF THIS CHRISTMAS

"NO REST BUT THE GRAVE FOR THE PILGRIM OF LOVE."

COPYRIGHT

An American Christmas Card. It is a Christmas Card of the
worst possible taste.

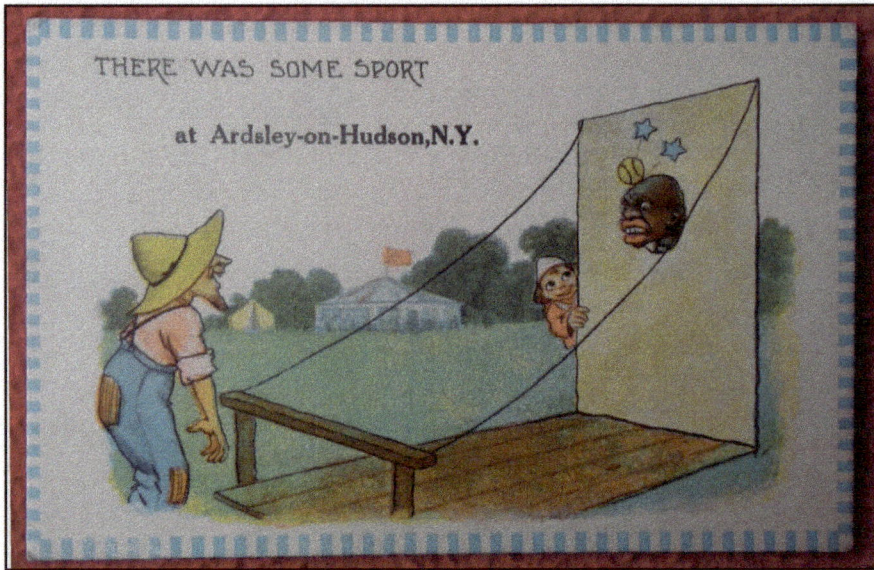

Above card was posted in 1912 at Ardsley-on-Hudson, New York.

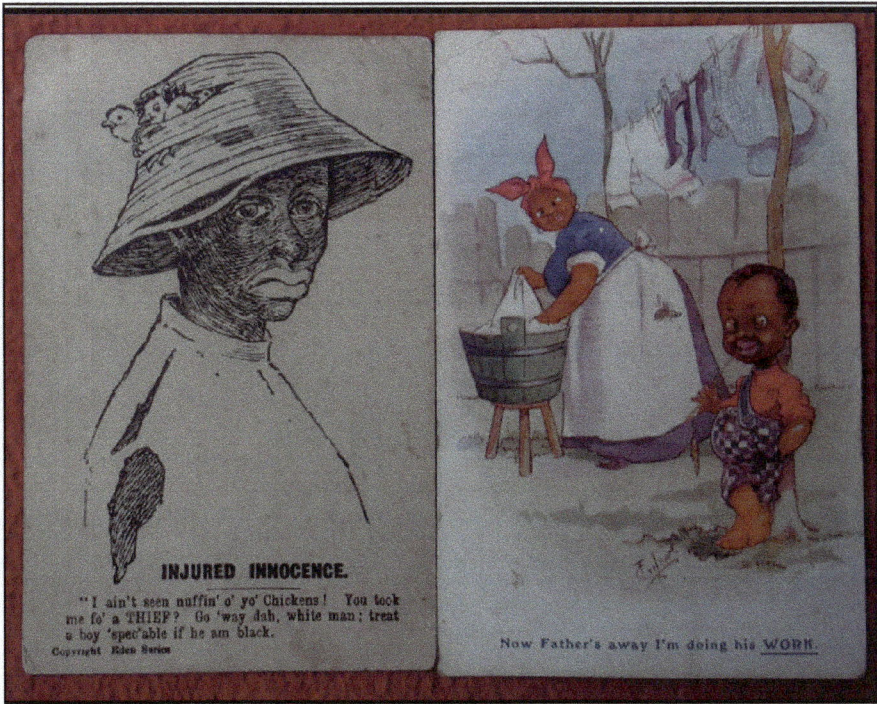

Injured innocence was British. Posted 1911.

The bottom card was posted in Erie, Pennsylvania in 1907.

Git a move on -- git a move on,
Dark clouds am passin' by.

Published by Moore & Gibson Co. N.Y.

British, Tuck series, not posted.

It's the little things in life that Coun

Published by Moore & Gibson Co N.Y.

American postcard, posted at Ocuqui,September 11th 1906.

Ma jolie Marraine, j'ai un aveu à vous faire... je suis nègre. 2654
My dear little godmother I must tell you something... I am a nigger.
Долженъ Вамъ признаться что... я негръ.

A French Card, not posted.
From the look of the puttees I think it was published in WW1.

British postcard. This was by Florence Kate Upton. Followed by three pictures that were taken from books and framed.

Florence Kate Upton was an American-born English cartoonist and author who created the Golliwog character, featured in a series of children's books. She also produced many paintings in a similar style.

Born: 22 February 1873 in New York, USA.
Died: 16 October 1922, London.
Education: The Art Students League of New York

The next three pictures are by Florence Upton and were taken from books and Framed.

FLORENCE UPTON PICTURES

Le plus joli brun
du régiment

The most
beautiful dack
one of regiment

FRENCH POSTCARD. NOT POSTED.

GERMAN POSTCARDS.

These cards were printed with the Cromolithograph printing system so are probably from pre WW1.

The third postcard, the man with the umbrella is also embossed and was posted in 1918.

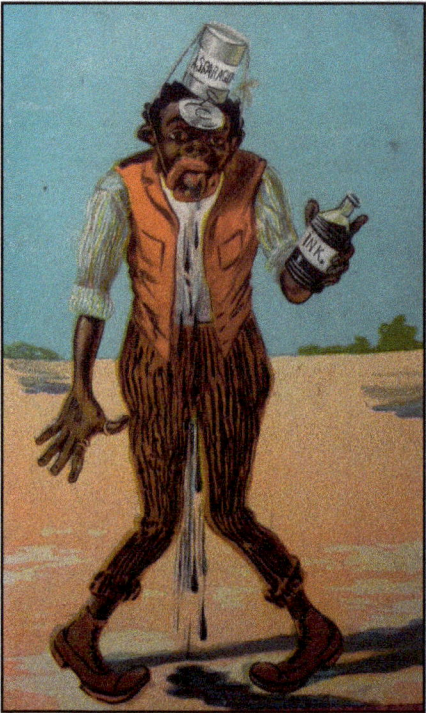

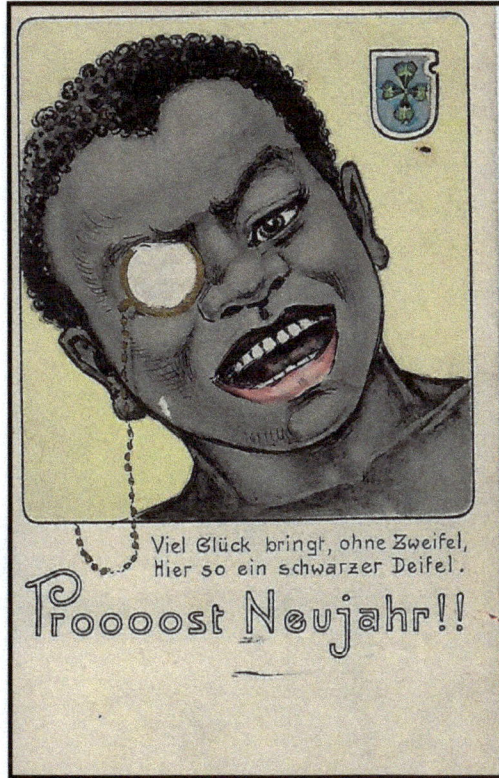

Viel Glück bringt, ohne Zweifel,
Hier so ein schwarzer Deifel.
Proooost Neujahr!!

The above postcard is German. It was not posted But I believe it is dated from around 1900.

The translation as near as I can get is-
Good luck. Without a doubt. Here is a black? Devil or Satan. 'HAPPY NEW YEAR!

American, Boston 1911. This card is embossed and also printed with the Cromolithograph printing system.

Posted at Raisin in California November 23rd 1891.
This card is embossed and Chromolithograph printing.

STAR SHOE STORE 1883. Reading, Pennsylvania.

British postcard, not posted.

British postcard posted Portsmouth December 1905

Two British postcards above posted July 1909 and 1913 below.

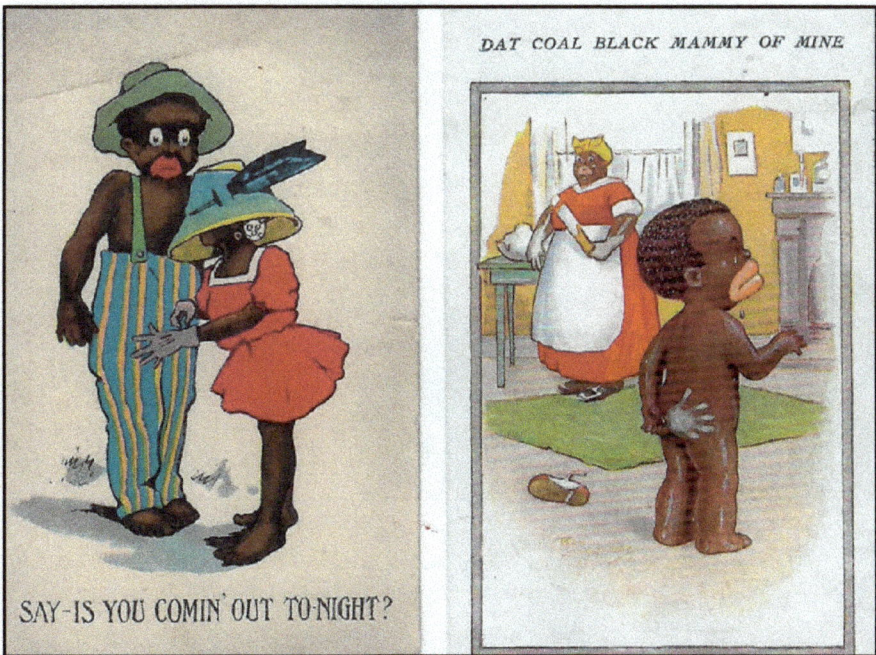

SAY·IS YOU COMIN' OUT TO·NIGHT?

DAT COAL BLACK MAMMY OF MINE

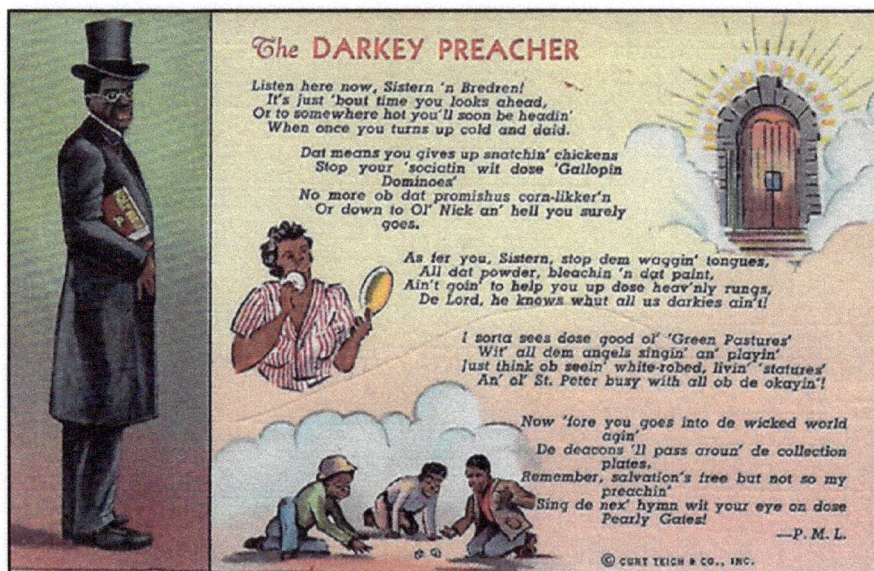

The top card is British, Jan 10th 1910. The bottom card is American, Chicago 1910.

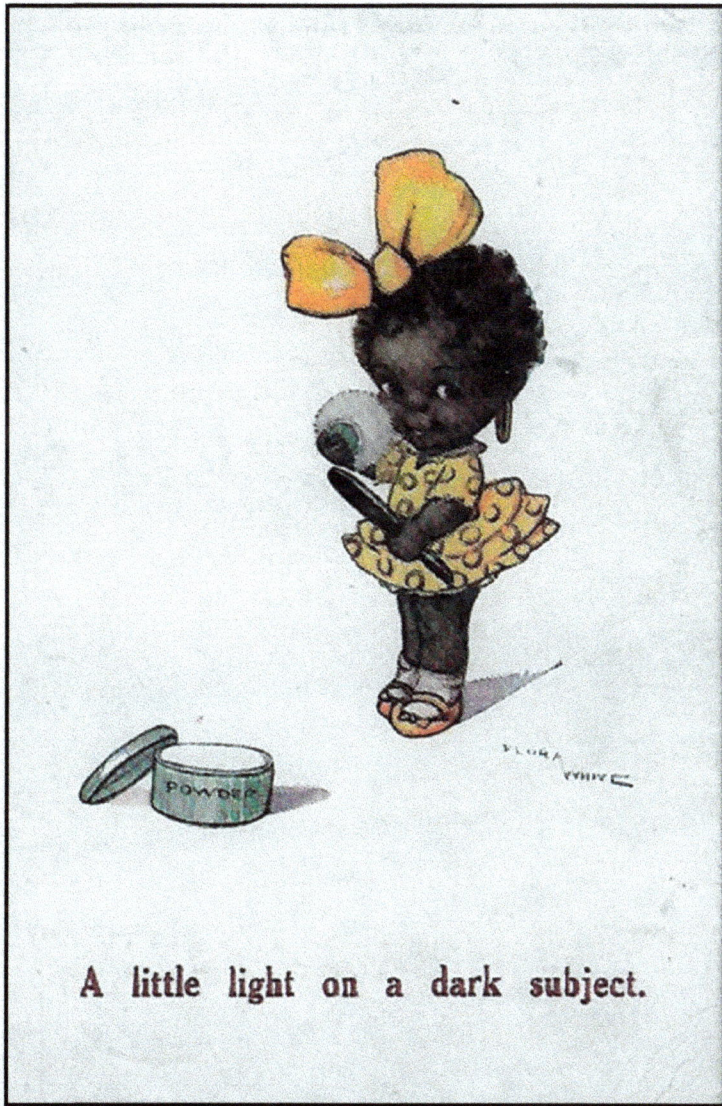

A little light on a dark subject.

British Postcard. Posted Southhampton 1921.

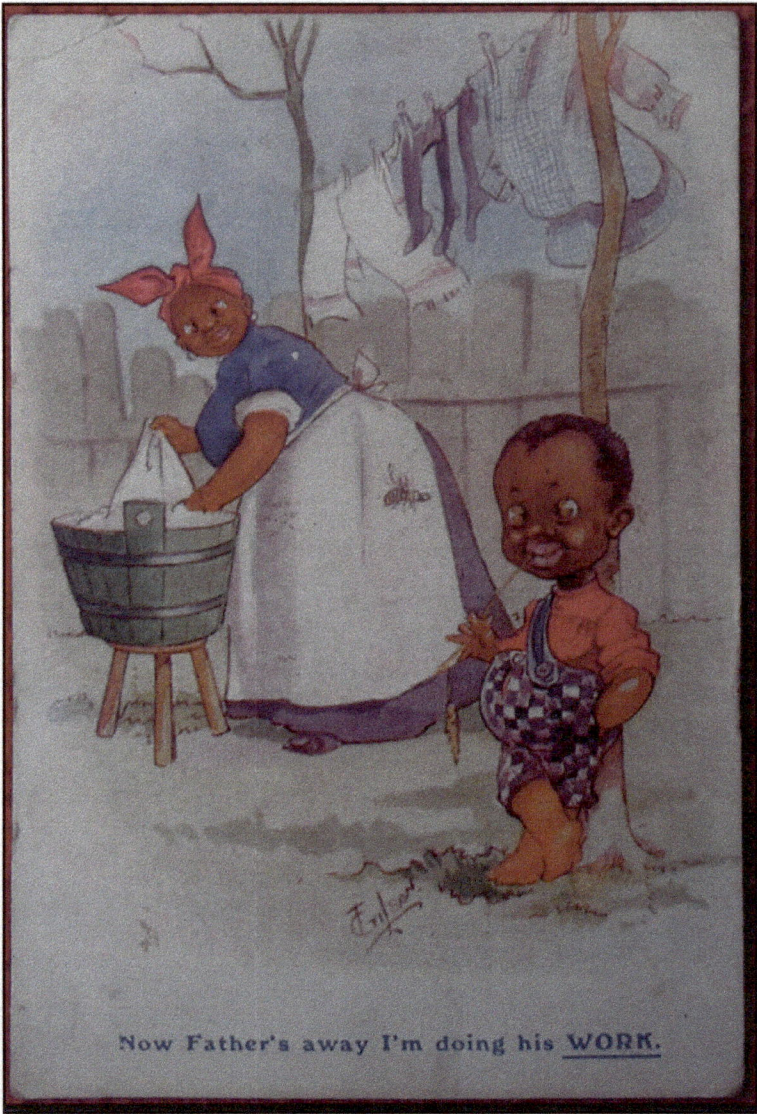

Now Father's away I'm doing his WORK.

American postcard, not posted.

British card, posted Brighton 1912.

FRIDAY.

British posted Truro 17th February 1924.

A Driol Liquer bottle. The drummer. Italian.

A Driol Liquer bottle. The water carrier. Italian.

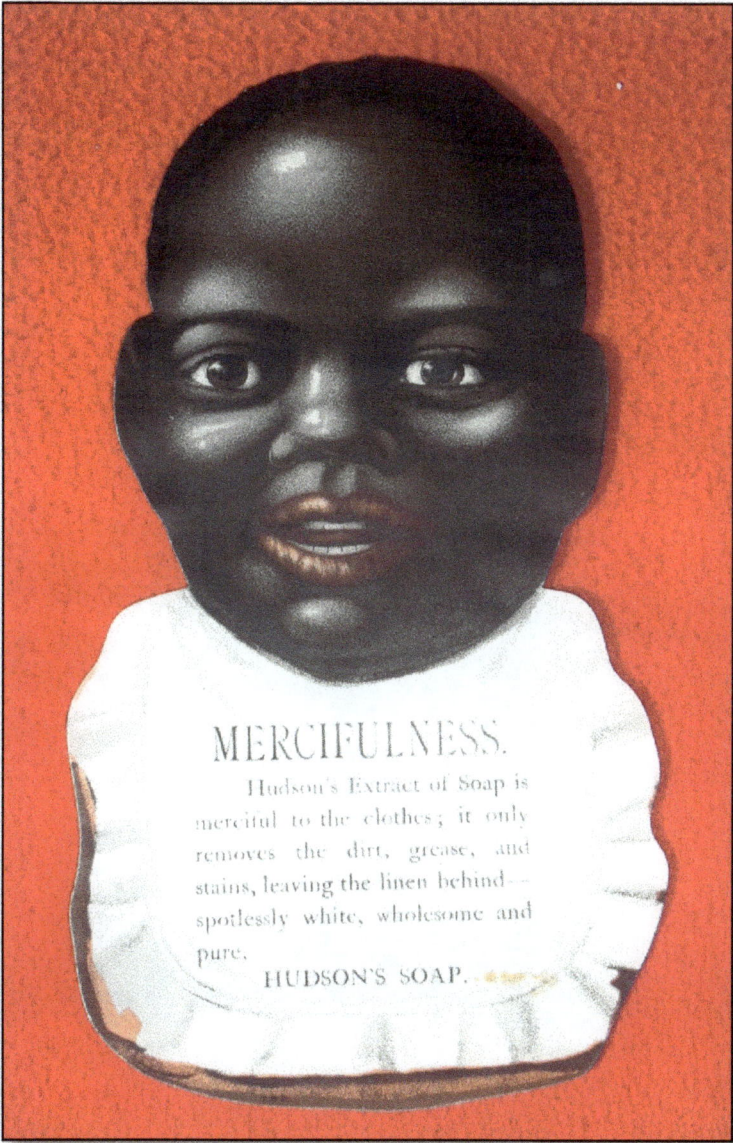

A BOX OF NICE SMELLING SOAP WITH A NOT SO NICE
THEME.

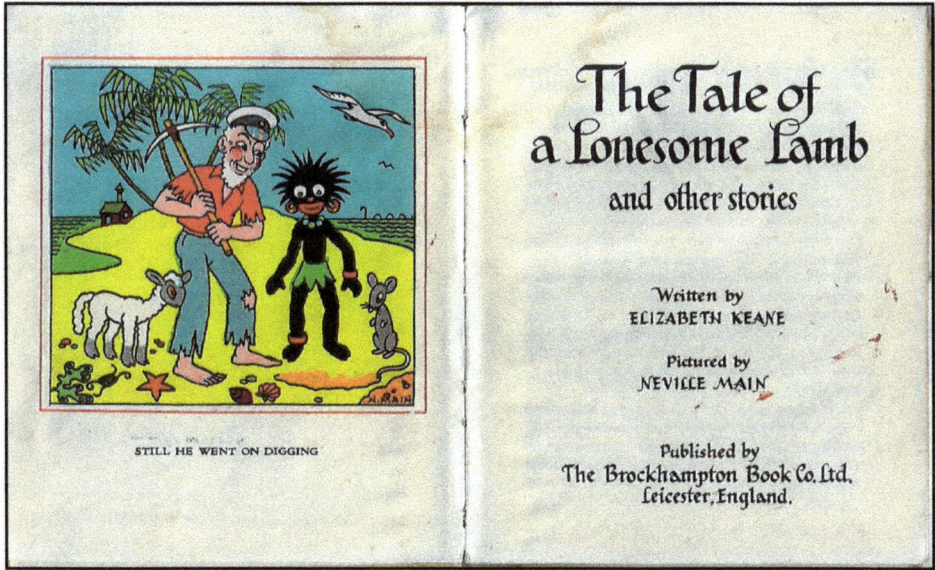

The Tale of
a Lonesome Lamb
and other stories

Written by
ELIZABETH KEANE

Pictured by
NEVILLE MAIN

Published by
The Brockhampton Book Co. Ltd.
Leicester, England.

STILL HE WENT ON DIGGING

This little book was published in 1944 and was written for small children. Fairy tales about the lamb a mouse and a South Sea Islander that were in a shop window. For ten to 12 year olds.

While researching for this little book I read about the following museum. I was very impressed and yet saddened by the stories behind the artifacts that have been collected and the difficulties that the people had in creating this museum.

The National Museum of African American History and Culture is a Smithsonian Institution museum located on the National Mall in Washington, D.C., in the United States. It was established in December 2003 and opened its permanent home in September 2016 with a ceremony led by President Barack Obama.

Smithsonian National African American Museum
1400 Constitution Ave. NW, Washington, DC 20560, United States

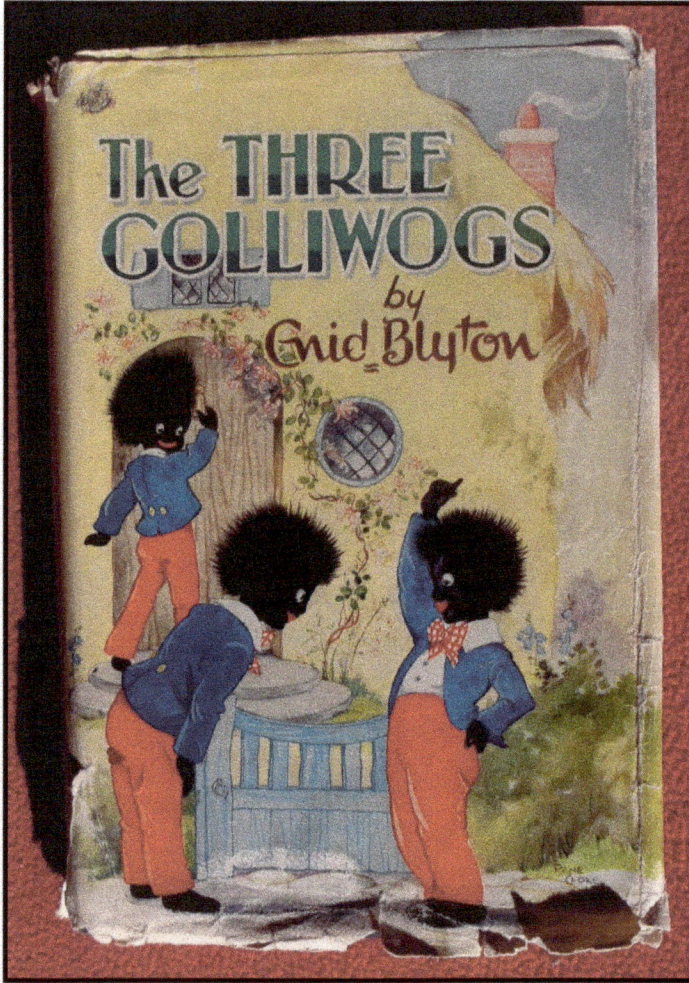

A Book by the children's writer Enid Blyton, 1897-1965.
She wrote 762 books in her life, sometimes writing
under the nom de plume 'Mary Pollock'.

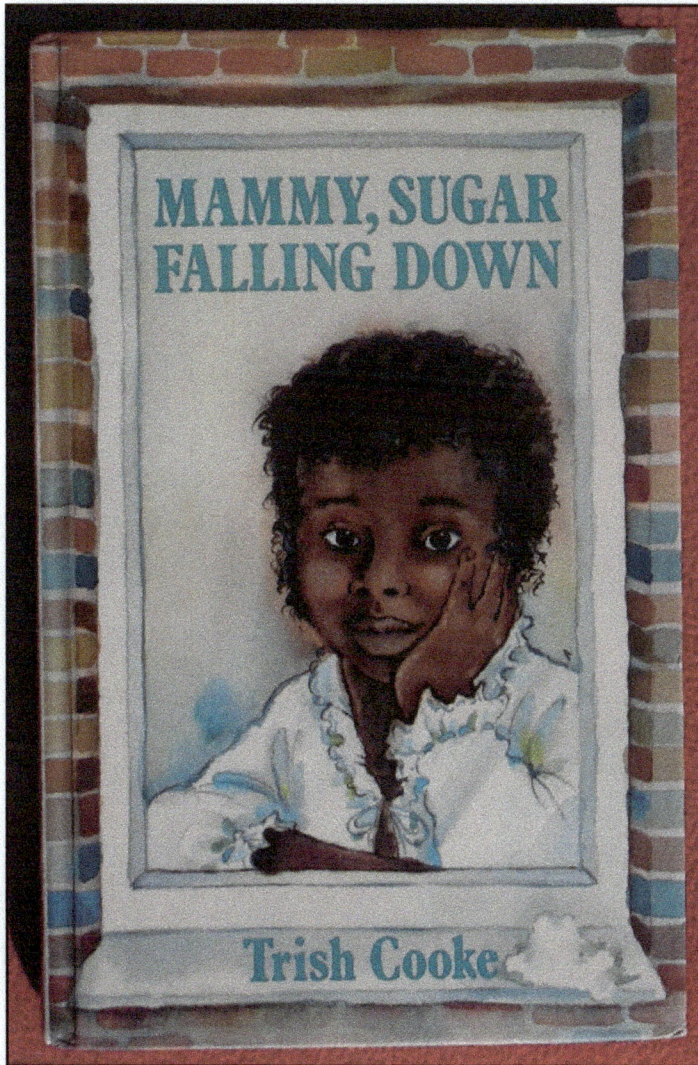

MAMMY, SUGAR
FALLING DOWN

Trish Cooke

A childs early reading book.

MUSIC FOR ALL
WITH WHICH IS INCORPORATED
"RADIO MUSIC"
1/- NET

FLORENCE MILLS

Gutenberg

£350 IN PRIZES Inside

The Music and Pictures of
"BLACK-BIRDS"
at THE PAVILION THEATRE
LONDON
No. 52. Vol. 9.

5 COMPLETE RADIO MUSIC PIECES
"I Want to Dance · · · · Fox Trot
Little Dream Lady · · · · Song
"Starlight · · · · Fox Trot
"Rapture · · · · Waltz
Three Dale Dances (Part 1) · · Piano
"WITH UKULELE ACCOMPANIMENT

A London Show magazine of the music and pictures of the participants, It features Florence Mills, singers, and dancers.

The show entitled The Black Birds' opened in November 1926 at the London Pavilion Music Hall with Florence Mills as the main attraction.

116

quaffing whatever beverage they may partake of in those quarters, and then somebody asking for a song. In remotest England they will oblige with "That Certain Party," or, if they are a little out of date, "Valencia." On the Mississippi, where they are a little more civilised, they break forth with something soft and crooning about Alabama moons that rhyme with piccaninny coons, and such pleasant nonsense. But at this particular Mississippi inn, the arrival of Levee Gang, plunderers of the river steamers, set the dear old mammies and papas into an advanced state of hysteria, with the result that the languorous melodies are exchanged for a vigorous fox trot song. "The Levee Gang," sung by Florence Mills as the leader of the bad bold robbers who are sending poor old President Coolidge quite pale with alarm up at the White House.

CHICK HORSEY AND GWENDOLYN GRAHAM IN THEIR DUET, "HOTTENTROT," A CHEEKY AND VERY BRIGHT NUMBER

FLORENCE MILLS AS THE INTRUDER IN "ARABELLA'S WEDDING-DAY."

A MERRY GROUP OF "PLANTATION TROTTERS," WITH CHICK HORSEY IN "HOTTENTROT."

coloured quarter, with Florence scintillating at their head. Blasé New Yorkers, stiff with dollars and satiated with excitement, forgot even Earl Carrol and the Ziegfeld Follies, in their amazement. Finally the "Blackbirds" came to Paris, that gay and naughty suburb of the U.S.A., and repeated their success. From Paris they came to London, the scene of Florence Mills' former triumph, opening at the London Pavilion amongst scenes of unprecedented enthusiasm. Now they are here in our midst. One of the gayest, most thrilling and original productions that has ever reminded us that the Negroes have other ways of spending their time than by singing doleful spirituals.

"THE BUTCHER"
(TINY RAY).
"THE BAKER"
(U. S. THOMPSON).
"THE CANDLESTICK MAKER"
(CHAS. WOODY).

A PLEASING TRIO AND MISS MILLS, THE BIRTHDAY CAKE SURPRISE.

A "STILL" OF "THE THREE EDDIES" IN "A LOT OF NONSENSE."
(TINY RAY, CHICK HORSEY AND CHAS. WOODY.)

FLORENCE MILLS AND COMPANY IN THE SENTIMENTAL INTERLUDE, "SILVER ROSE."

THE LONDON PAVILION MUSIC HALL

November 1926 saw the opening of 'Black Birds' at the Pavilion. This was followed by the opening of 'One Dam Thing After Another' on May the 20th 1927. On March the 22nd 1928.'This Year of Grace' opened at the Pavilion and was followed by 'Lucky Girl' in January 1929, and 'Wake up and Dream' on March the 27th the same year. 1930 saw 'Cochran's Review of 1930 open, followed by 'Cochran's Review of 1931' the following year,

The London pavilion was on Shaftesbury Avenue, Westminster, London. It opened in 1859, converted to use as a cinema in April 1934 and closed in 1986. It is now called' The Trocadero.'

A carved tobacco pipe.

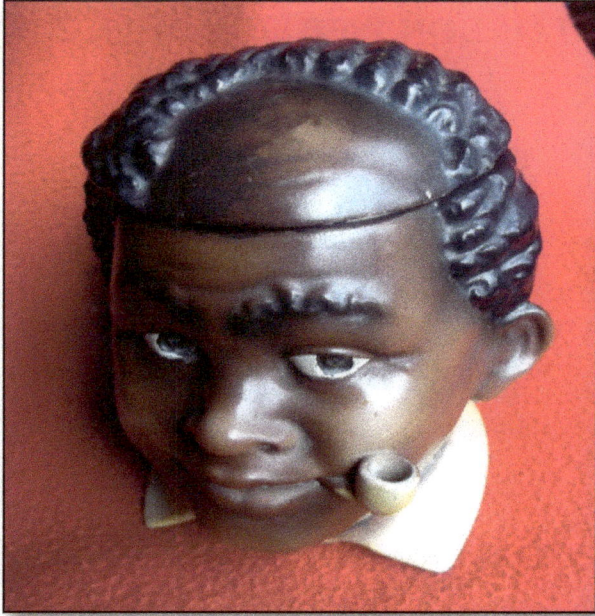

A tobacco jar, made in USA. Man with pipe.

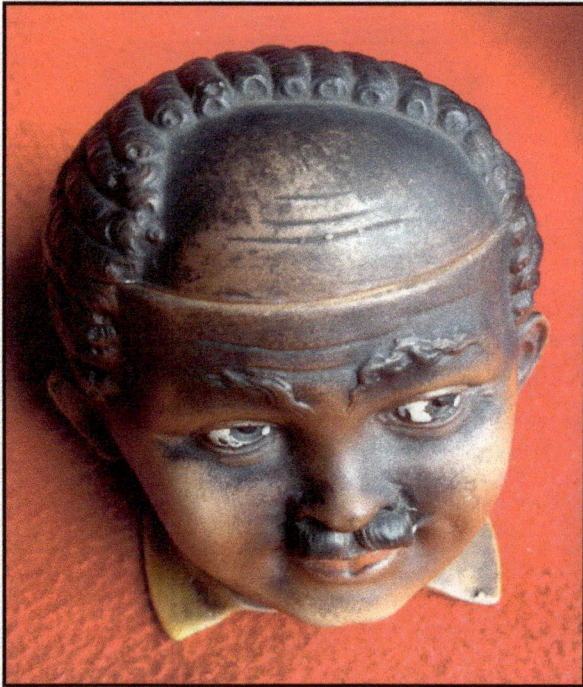

Tobacco jar, made in USA. Man with moustache.

Tobacco Jar, made in USA. A girl with a scarf.

Above is a biscuit or cookie jar.

This is not a crested china piece but created by
VILLEROY & BOSH.

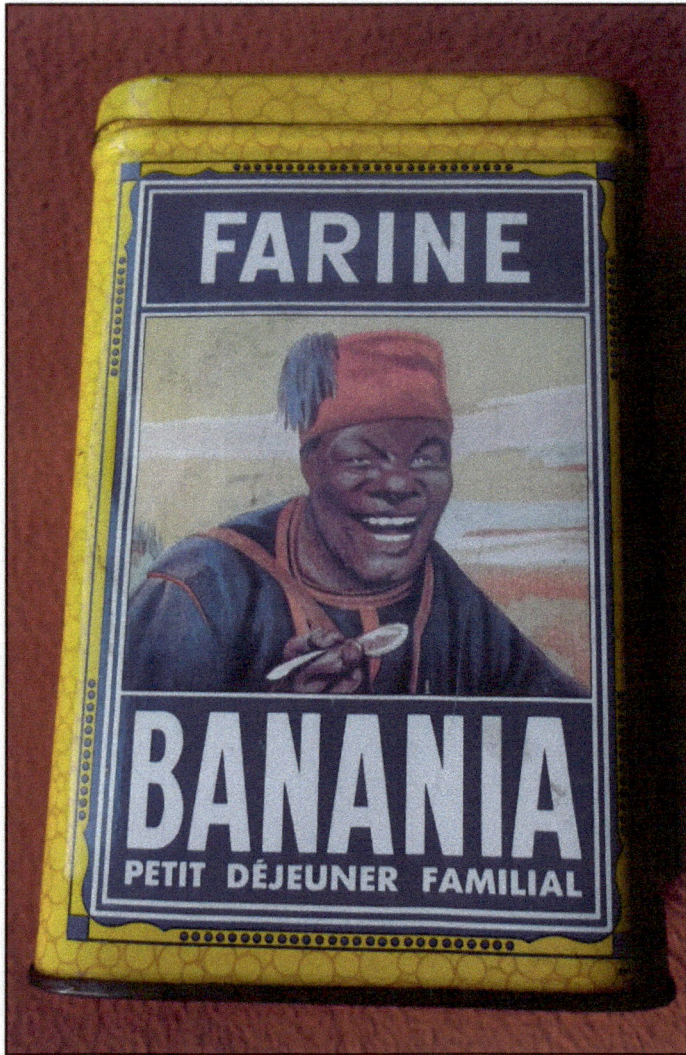

A French flour tin.

French chocolate powder & American tin lids.

Arcadian Crested China ' A little Study in Black and Fright.
There are various versions of this.

THE BLACK AND WHITE MINSTREL SHOW

The Black and White Minstrel Show opened at the Victoria Palace Theatre on the 25th May 1962, that is coming up to 60 years ago.

Another version called The Magic of the Minstrels ran for three years.

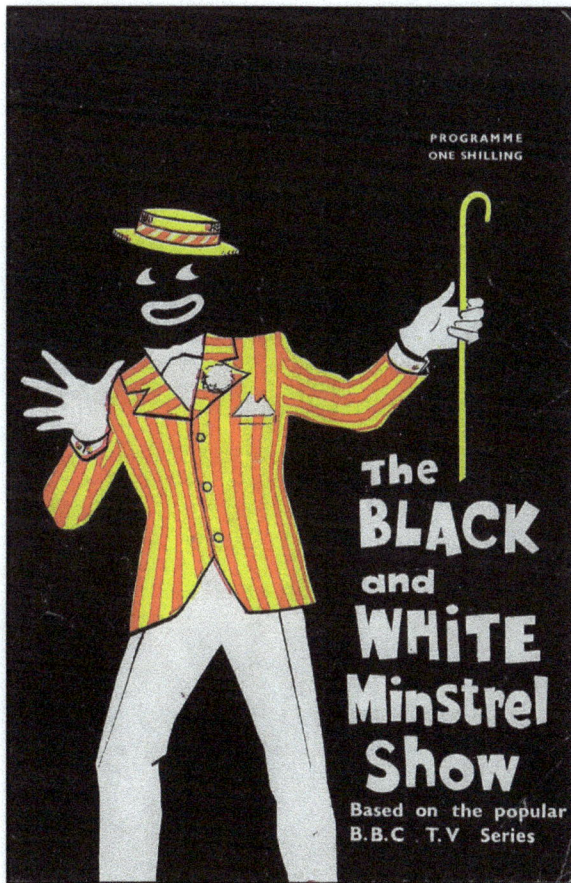

LESLIE A. MACDONNELL announces that
ROBERT LUFF HOLDINGS LTD. in assoc. with GEORGE MITCHELL
present

The Black and White Minstrel Show

George Steele conducts the Victoria Palace Orchestra in
THE MINSTREL OVERTURE

First performance
Friday, May 25th, 1962

1 The George Mitchell Minstrels and Maids and the Television Toppers
   " ON PARADE "

2 TONY MERCER, THE MINSTRELS and "An Old Soft Shoe"

3 LESLIE CROWTHER, MARGO HENDERSON and
   GEORGE CHISHOLM in "A Three Point Landing"

4 MEET THE GIRLS

5 GEORGE CHISHOLM and THE JAZZERS with PAT ELLIS

6 DAI FRANCIS pays Tribute to AL JOLSON

7 MARGO HENDERSON ... ... The Essence of Versatility

8 THE MINSTRELS MAIDS and TOPPERS say
   "We'll Si Si you in Bahia "

INTERMISSION

9 HOORAY FOR HOLLYWOOD !

10 THE SCHALLER BROTHERS ... International Comedy Trampolinists

11 TONY MERCER and THE BOYS and GIRLS take you
    " Down Memory Lane "

12 THE JAYE SISTERS

13 COWBOYS and INDIANS !

14 SPEED MANIACS—LESLIE CROWTHER and GEORGE CHISHOLM

15 JOHN BOULTER, THE MINSTRELS, MAIDS and TOPPERS in
    " Serenade in the Night "

16 LESLIE CROWTHER assisted by PAT ELLIS invites you to
    " Listen with Mother "

17 THE MINSTRELS ... ... " Dry Bones "

18 THE COMPANY ... ... " Doo Dah Dey "

THE GEORGE MITCHELL MINSTRELS
Featured Soloists:
TONY MERCER, DAI FRANCIS, JOHN BOULTER
Maurice Arthur, John Van Best, Jan Bolitho, Steve Bryce,
Donald Cleaver, Glyn Dawson, Malcolm Dockeray, Patric
Feeney, David Hartley, George Holden, Alan Hollidge, Arthur
Lewis, Norman Rich, Michael Rowlatt, Alan Starkey, Ron
Urquhart.

THE TELEVISION TOPPERS
Heather Angus, Jill Bradburn, Rita Compton, Sandra Fingerhut,
Daphne Ford, Jan Gummer, Diane Hastings, Elspeth Handy,
Judy Mackenzie, Kay Matthews, Dorothy Nichol, Penny Rigden.

THE MITCHELL MAIDS
Ruth Baker, Tina Brown, Velta Cakizis, Angela Langton,
Mary Moss, Elizabeth Paul.

THE JAZZERS
Jim Easton, Clinton ffrench, John Gordon, Jackie MacHardie,
Tiny Winters.

I often wondered why the producer did not employ any black singers?

For I had been to the cinema when I was about 10yrs old and heard Paul Robeson sing the Canoe Song in the 1935 film 'Sanders Of the River' so much so, that as I grew up I bought his records.

NATIONAL MUSEUM OF AFRICAN AMERICAN HISTORY AND CULTURE

The National Museum of African American History and Culture is a Smithsonian Institution museum located on the National Mall in Washington, D.C., in the United States. It opened in September of 2016. President Obama led the opening ceremony.

Address: 1400 Constitution Ave. NW, Washington, DC 20560, USA.

This is a fine museum that collects artifacts that represent the milestones paving the path in the history of the African American people.

Note I read about the above museum in the National Geographic magazine and found that they listed thirteen destinations in the USA for learning about the history and culture of the African American people.

BIBLIOGRAPHY

SMITHSONIAN NATIONAL AFRICAN MUSEUM
Smithsonian National African American Museum
1400 Constitution Ave. NW, Washington, DC 20560,
United States.
www.nationalgeographic.org>encyclopedia>kingdom

"THEY TREATED US ROYALLY" The experiences of
black Americans in Britain during the Second World
War | Imperial War Museums (iwm.org.uk)

TUSKEGEE UNIVERSITY
Facts provided by Tuskegee Airmen Inc. and
the Tuskegee University Office of Marketing and
Communications.
Tuskegee University: Home www.tuskegee.edu

RED BALL EXPRESS.
Red Ball Express - Wikipedia
en.wikipedia.org › wiki › Red_Ball_Express

MARCHAND MISSION (FRENCH)
From Wikipedia.

THE UIGHARS
Ref. https://www.bbc.co.uk/news/world-asia-
china-22278037

ROMANI/GYPSY: a member of a people originating in
South Asia and traditionally having an itinerant way of
life and speaking a language (Romani) that is related to
Hindi. Google

WIZARD COMIC. Chick Gordon - Lambiek
Comiclopedia

BILLY IRELAND CARTOON LIBRARY & MUSEUM

There is a museum in America for cartoons and
caricatures in Comic Art. It was established in 1977. It
is at Ohio State University Libraries at Columbus, Ohio.
The address: 1813 N High St, Columbus. OH 43210
USA.
The website is: cartoons.osu.edu

www.ingramcontent.com/pod-product-compliance
Lightning Source LLC
Chambersburg PA
CBHW051617030426
42334CB00030B/3232